JESUS—
THE JEW'S JEW

JESUS—THE JEW'S JEW

Zola Levitt

CREATION HOUSE
Carol Stream, Illinois

© 1973 by Creation House. All rights reserved. Printed in the United States of America. Published by Creation House, 499 Gundersen Drive, Carol Stream, Illinois 60187.

Scriptural quotations taken from the *New American Standard Bible*, with permission of the Lockman Foundation, LaHabre, California.

Library of Congress Catalog Card Number: 73-86271
International Standard Book Number: 0-88419-064-1

To Tom McCall,
devoted friend and able missionary to the Jews

Contents

1

Jesus Is Jewish

Let's face it.

Jesus is Jewish.

He always was and He always will be. He never "converted" to anything.

But it almost seems as though this fact is something to be spoken of in whispers. How could God's Son be one of *them?* How could the very founder of Christianity, that great *"non-Jewish"* religion, get away with being Jewish?

Christians know He is Jewish and many of them even like it. I did hear of one, however, who said, "If that's really true I don't think I can have real respect for Him even though He's my Savior."

And as for the Jews, they don't think He "looks Jewish." As I know them (and I know them—I'm one of them) they don't think He makes a "good Jewish" Messiah.

You see, there's Jewish and then there's *Jewish*. The important thing about "Jewishness" is a kind of style. Gentiles just don't have it.

But personally, I think Jesus had plenty of it. By me He's Jewish.

One of my favorite moments in the New Testament is the dialogue between Jesus and Nathanael in the first chapter of John. It really shows a Jewish spirit and humor. I don't hear it quoted much because I think a lot of Christians miss the flavor of it.

Here comes Nathanael to the Lord, very skeptical. Philip has told him that the Messiah has come, and out of a little village called Nazareth. Nathanael carps, "Can any good thing come out of Nazareth?" He doesn't like small towns, and he doesn't think the Messiah has really come. Those are both Jewish tendencies.

The Lord gives him a greeting that indicates that He has some special knowledge about Nathanael, even though He's never met him.

They talk only a moment and Nathanael is convinced that Jesus is the Messiah indeed. He is astonished when the Lord says, "I knew you already when you were sitting under that fig tree where Philip found you."

Then comes the line I'd put in my special collection of Jesus' Greatest Hits: "Because I said to you that I saw you under the fig tree, do you believe? You shall see greater things than these . . . you shall see the heavens opened, and the angels of God ascending and descending upon the Son of Man" (John 1:50,51).

Talk about getting the last word!

Now that's a really Jewish line—"You like fig tree tricks? Well, you ain't seen nothin' yet!"

But Jesus' "Jewishness" is not limited to His personal characteristics; He evidences it in many other ways in the Gospels.

He has, foremost, that hard-headed courage of the Jew, who can be beaten down but never defeated. He is the very image of the longsuffering Jewish nation, so unfairly matched against a relentless host of antagonists and yet always surviving them.

He is Jewish because He talks like a Jewish prophet. He speaks with the broad authority of Ezekiel or Isaiah. And He speaks intimately of the Father like Moses or Abraham.

And He speaks with complete respect for those great patriarchs, demonstrating that He is not out to replace Judaism.

He also has a Jewish regard for a fine meal, a well-run business enterprise, a non-adulterous marriage.

He is Jewish because He acted like a Jew. He obeyed God's commandments com-

11

pletely. He celebrated each Jewish feast. Christians tend not to notice that our Lord regarded the festivals ordained by God in Leviticus 23 as vital in His own life, yet He certainly did.

We see in John 7 that our Lord made the arduous trip from Galilee to Jerusalem, through country where He was a wanted man, to commemorate the Feast of Tabernacles. He had to go on foot and in secret, skirting hostile Samaria. The walk was nearly one hundred miles!

Why would He go to that trouble? Was He some sort of diplomat trying to please the Pharisees of the Temple? Did He think His ministry needed a little public relations work?

Hardly. If you want to know why He went through that, ask a Jew. A Jew knows what Tabernacles means to another Jew.

And Jesus sat down to celebrate Passover with His disciples when He had only hours before Calvary. What would you do tonight if you knew you were going on trial for your life at dawn?

Why would Jesus Christ, whose very hours were numbered, stop to observe a holiday?

Ask a Jew. A Jew knows what Passover means to another Jew.

In the case of the Feast of Dedication, Christ celebrated a patriotic national holiday (Chanukah). That is, this festival was not one of those required by God but was

12

instituted to commemorate the rededication of the Second Temple by the Jews in 165 B.C.

In other words, He was so much a Jew that He joined, at great danger, an Israeli festival. Certain Jewish practices (like certain Christian practices) are not scriptural but have been ordained by earthly spiritual leaders down through the ages. Jesus observed those as well.

When I first picked up the New Testament I didn't have to read very far to see that Jesus was Jewish. In fact I had to read only the first verse. Matthew 1:1 presents the Lord as "the son of David, the son of Abraham."

If that's not a Jew they're talking about I don't know who is!

Clearly, if the Chosen People fully understood that Jesus is a "Jew's Jew," they would more quickly recognize Him as their Messiah. Surely it's one of the most tragic paradoxes of human history that God's supreme gift to His exalted nation has been all but lost to them.

The fault seems to be divided. I know a lot of unreasonable Jews who won't stand still for the facts of the Gospel out of pure prejudice. But then I know a lot of ignorant Christians who curse the Jews, and thus defame God's will (Genesis 12:3).

I'm not taking sides. This book isn't written to Jews or non-Jews particularly, but to those who love God. I'm in the position of having been up and down this street and, if you'll forgive me, I'm going to kind of cut loose on the whole situation.

I was raised really Jewish ("Oy, have I got a girl for you!") and I now follow my Messiah Jesus. Call me a Hebrew Christian or a Messianic Jew or whatever you like; the truth set me free and I want to explain what I found out.

I don't feel merely "inspired" to bring my people to Christ; I'm a *maniac* about it! But it really is a hard thing to do.

The Jewish view is that Christ was not the Messiah. He was in no way comparable to Abraham, Isaac, and Jacob, whose spiritual graces He should have far exceeded; and He doesn't look like a Jew, talk like a Jew, or deliver the Jews from their troubles.

The Jew takes the position that the prophecies relating to Christ have been misinterpreted or interpolated after the events of His ministry. So much for the Old Testament. As for the New Testament, the Jew does not regard it as the Word of God.

And that's that.

Furthermore, the Jew feels spiritually superior to any Gentile. Is he not one of God's Chosen? Has he not outlasted the Egyptians, Babylonians, Romans, Germans, and practically everybody else? Are not his traditions established long before the upstart Christianity—intact after millennia? Doesn't he eat better food, marry better, conduct more profitable business, and tell better jokes than the Gentile?

To this spiritually secure and earthly-successful Chosen Person comes the Baptist church member on his visitation duties, or the smooth-cheeked Campus Crusader with his little booklet on salvation.

It's hopeless. The Jew (1) doesn't think he needs to be saved, (2) thinks the New Testament is a fabrication, and (3) doesn't like *goyim* (Gentiles).

Yet, in increasing numbers, Jews are coming to Christ.

The Lord said it would happen, and it truly demonstrates His power.

Probably the biggest factor in the Jew finally coming around is his realization that he can receive his Messiah and still remain a Jew. Because of less than heaven-inspired efforts to "convert" the Jew by force in the past, he has traditionally thought of "conversion" as going over to the enemy. A "converted Jew" was a traitor—up until this generation.

But today's evangelical Christian is learning to make the Jew welcome in the church; he is seeing that Jews make pretty good Christians.

And why not? Is it so strange for a Jew to love his brother, to worship one God, to follow the teachings of his ancestors?

Instead of preaching hellfire and damnation at the Jew, as Christians have through the centuries, today's witness for Christ is realizing that the Lord, and all His disciples, and all His apostles, were Jews. Instead of regarding the Jew as some kind of infidel, the Christian who has read the Bible is realizing that he and the Jew are "one in Christ."

It's a far cry from the days when the armed Christian hordes of Europe came to rout the Jews out of the Holy Land. Who was taking whose Promised Land from whom?

Now that the end times are coming around, the Lord has inspired His followers to share their faith in a different way. With the historicity of the New Testament firmly established, people are becoming interested in what happened back then. They are seeing that Christianity used to be Jewish. They are realizing that the Messiah who said, "Salvation is of the Jew," chose Jews to send His Gospel to the world.

They are hearkening back to a time when it was strange for a Gentile Christian to come to church. They are remembering the apostles having to point out, "You don't have to be Jewish to love Christ." They are remembering that Peter, that completely Jewish servant of the Messiah, was shocked at the prospect of taking Christ's precious gift of salvation to non-Jews.

And the Jews, for their part, appreciate this change in approach. A Hebrew Christian is a man at peace. He has a wonderful heritage—he was chosen and his father was chosen, and his father's father—and he is loved, as only a true Christian can love, by his Gentile Christian neighbor.

Jews don't hate Christ. It is erroneous to think of the Jew as prejudiced against "another religion." It is a principle of Jewish law that everyone may worship as he pleases. It is a testimony to that principle that, at this time in Israel, the detested Arabs are allowed free passage to their Dome of the Rock temple in the Old City in Jerusalem.

The Jew is not prejudiced, but he is touchy. He doesn't like to be called a "Christ-killer." He remembers that Christ forgave the Romans who crucified Him and finds it a poor testimony to meet an unforgiving Christian. The Jew is earthy and practical. He goes by what he sees. He is less likely to receive Christ on the Lord's merits than on the merits of the Christians he sees around him.

Jews don't blaspheme Jesus. Some defensively question whether the Lord ever really came, but none call Him an out-and-out fake. Those willing to take up the Gospel open-mindedly are surprised to find a very Jewish, very pleasing personality in Christ.

Reading the Gospels, the Jew can find the arguments between Christ and the Rabbis of His time. The content of those arguments make the Rabbis look unfair, overbearing, blasphemous, even "un-Jewish." The Jew gets the uncomfortable feeling that he has been following those Rabbis, whereas the other guy—Jesus—won the arguments.

When the Jew does become a follower of Jesus, there is still a battle. He can rest comfortable in the assurance of everlasting life, but the Jew insists on a meaningful earthly existence as well. The Jew is a creature of feelings, and he wants to feel *good*.

He goes to a church luncheon with *goyisha* businessmen and gets uncomfortable. First of all, the *goyim* get there on time, ready to eat. Isn't lunch supposed to be a little late? What's the rush?

Then the ham and cheese come out.

The saved Jew knows he can eat the ham now. If he's a typical Jew he's eaten it before. But that doesn't mean he *likes* it. The simple fare at the church is a far cry from Mama's chicken soup and marvelous cheese blintzes.

Ham is okay, but "pastrami it ain't."

Then there's the Bible study—a circle of Gentiles all listening to one teacher. Jews don't like "experts" in the Word. They have a tradition: when something God said isn't quite clear they get with a group of good Jewish neighbors and sit down every night for ten or fifteen years and hash it out.

Where are those time-honored, good-humored arguments over what God means by what He says? Doctrine is okay, but Jewish it ain't.

Then there's God Himself. The Jew knows Him well. Nobody has ever had to instruct the Jew about God. Christians seem to love to go over the Epistles; to quote those apostles on how we should do things. To the Jew this is no better than his old 613 laws. Paul is okay, but God he ain't.

It's the little things. The Jew gets in a bind because he feels as though he has to make changes. And he feels as though he knew how to live just fine before all these "new-fangled" Christian practices came along. Christian dating patterns, worship on Sunday, witnessing, bookstores devoted entirely to religious books, woefully unimpressive weddings and funerals, so-so music in the services, surprise visits from church members and pastors, no smoking, praying in your own words with an uncovered head—all are entirely new to the Jew.

Christianity is okay, but Jewish it ain't.

Needless to say the magnificent blessings of the Lord soon make up the differences and the Jew, like any Christian, experiences the wonder of abundant life in Him.

Jesus proves to be a good Jewish Messiah.

All of this just sort of outlines the problems involved in bringing the Jew to Jesus and into fellowship with Jewish and Gentile Christians. That Christ is an adequate Messiah for the Jew, and that He delights in saving and sustaining the Jew, we know already. That the Jew will come to the Lord and stay with Him we can see.

But just to gain a real appreciation for this new "Jews for Jesus" movement— just to see what it really takes to convert the Jew to Jesus—we have to color in a genuine Jewish personality.

Let me introduce you to my father . . . .

2

My Father Died Unsaved

Abie: "It's so wonderful, to trust in the Messiah."

Nate: "But the Messiah hasn't come yet!"

Abie: "Trust I got!"

That was my father's position—short on assurance, long on faith.

You have to give credit where it's due: it's easier to have faith in a Savior who has come already than to wait on and on for one who hasn't.

Father spent a long and hectic life with the Gentile all around him. First he ran from the

Gentile; then he competed in business with him. But always, he avoided him as much as possible.

My father didn't know his age or his own birthday. He celebrated his birthday on Father's Day each year. When we buried him we called him seventy, because he looked at least that old.

He died unsaved, without the slightest knowledge that the Messiah had come. In seventy years no one had witnessed to my father. I don't wonder. He would have been a tough customer!

He was born in a little country town near Riga, Latvia. Latvia is just about gone now, swallowed up by Russia. I picture my father's hometown as looking something like Anatevka, the little village in *Fiddler on the Roof*.

My father's father was a shoemaker—not a shoe repairman, but an artist who made shoes to your measure. It took months to make a pair of shoes, each of the shoes different, of course, to conform exactly to your two different feet. They lasted years and years.

My father's memories of that little town were unclear after the years. When you've forgotten your birthday not much else remains. He did recall walking all day to go to the opera in Riga with his father, brothers, and sisters dying from flu and appendicitis, and, of course, always wearing the best of homemade shoes.

But he remembered most clearly the unrelenting persecutions of the Jews.

As a teenager my father decided to leave it all behind. The odds were not good in rural Latvia. If the flu didn't get you some ignorant policeman might crack your head open with his stick because you had a skullcap on it. Or the synagogue might be consumed in an unfortunate fire. Or soldiers might come through and your sisters would never make it home from market.

Sometimes after the turn of the century my father walked from Latvia to the Atlantic coast, across the entire breadth of Europe. *Sneaked* might be a better term, because my father kept himself hidden. He was a Jew, after all, surrounded by Gentiles in each country he passed through. He knew what a Gentile was—some kind of animal in human form who lived on Jewish blood.

This evaluation wasn't quite fair, but my father didn't know any differently from his experiences in Latvia.

I should add that the terms *Gentile* and *Christian* were exactly equal in my father's mind.

He didn't make the trip in one long walk, but stopped off wherever a community seemed safe enough for Jews. He remembered Zurich and Paris as pleasant stops. He seemed to remember a stopover of several weeks during which he took a night course at a university; it might have been in Zurich. He studied bookkeeping, a course that later was to come in handy.

The purpose of his trip was to discover some city where he might live without fear; however, he didn't find one in all of Europe. Each place he stopped he inquired, "Where is the Jewish community (ghetto)?" He had learned the question in Polish, Czech, German, French, and finally English. Anytime he got a derisive answer ("Our Jewish community is full—we don't need any more Jews") he moved on.

And he ended up all the way over here, in the U.S.A.

He came over in steerage on a ship that accepted Jews and transported them by the pound like freight.

In the New York harbor he asked the customs officer where the Jewish community was. He was sent to Grand Central Station to get a train. New York had plenty of Jews, the officer told him, and advised my father to go West.

My father had had enough train riding when he arrived at Pittsburgh. He got off the train, resolved to go no further. He asked about the Jewish community and was sent up the street a short distance from the

24

station into Pittsburgh's wholesale district on Fifth Avenue.

There he broke into tears. What a scene! Signs in Yiddish and Hebrew, a kosher meat store, tailors, skullcaps—it looked like a science-fiction Anatevka, with autos and streetcars in the familiar Jewish marketplace.

He walked into a clothes store and paid his life savings—three American dollars—for six neckties. He went out on the sidewalk in front of the store and, speaking only Yiddish, sold them to passers-by for one dollar each.

He was back in a short time asking for twelve neckties.

They hired him.

In three years he owned the company.

It was heavenly for my father to live in this country. Imagine being able to speak Yiddish in the streets without being spat upon! Imagine the policeman directing traffic on the corner—in all the years that good Irishman had stood there he had not killed a single Jew!

Imagine going to the synagogue on the Sabbath without fear of rocks coming through the windows!

This is not to say that father *liked* the Gentiles, or that the Gentiles liked the Jews. What could be expected from a Gentile except derision and hatred, after all? But still, peace was peace. Surely God had brought him to this great America.

Oh, he'd been called "dirty Jew" and "kike" plenty of times, but to the man from Riga this was practically a luxury. The Gentile didn't like the Jew—that was nature. Just so there were no pogroms.

His secret thought was that the Gentile was jealous because the Gentile was no tie salesman! He may have been right.

Father was in his early twenties when he took over the clothing company. He had reached his full height—five feet, three inches—carried a walking stick and wore a cape. He grew a smart moustache and bought a motorcar. In the Jewish community he was quite an eligible bachelor.

In his lifetime he dated only one girl, and he married her. He met my mother-to-be at a Jewish settlement house where he was on the program as a debater. He was debating the issue of prohibition with a local judge. I don't know what side Father took in that debate, but he never drank.

Sweet Adeline Yatkovsky was the pianist on the program, and when she played "The Star-Spangled Banner" my father's heart was won.

He didn't approach her, of course. The procedure in those days was to write a letter asking to visit at the home of the girl. Father picked out some good stationery and proceeded to woo.

Mother, of course, held the note for some two weeks before handing it over to her father, who replied to my father. He made suitable investigations, assuring himself of my father's religious convictions and financial soundness, and then stated that my father could call at their home at an appointed hour.

My father bought a new suit and cape, waxed his moustache, washed his motorcar, and practiced his English (Mother had been born in the New World).

At length he made his visit, promptly at the appointed time.

My mother did not enter the room for the first hour. If she had, she would have been thought a hussy! My father first had to talk with her father, and then her mother. Finally Adeline appeared on the staircase, holding a dainty hanky to her nose. It was highly fashionable in those days for the young lady to be a bit sick. She did not actually join the application procedure but had to be satisfied with glancing at my father over the hanky.

Apparently it was effective.

The first time he got her alone he proposed.

It was a weird marriage from my perspective. I was born some twenty years later and about all I saw was frantic love and frantic fighting. They would shout at each other in Yiddish, Hebrew, Polish, and I don't know what else, but then they would spend long Sundays together in their room.

But I saw what my father thought of her most emphatically one day. We were at the Miami airport; my father and I had gone on our summer vacation, leaving mother to "watch the store." She came down after a few weeks and father was to go back. When she got off the plane they fell into each other's arms and began kissing and kissing. I was mortified! I was about twelve years old, and I couldn't stand the embarrassment. Here were these two old people necking in this public place!

How could I ever show my face again?

Father sent money back to Latvia and one by one brought over his surviving brothers and sisters. By the time I was old enough to count relatives, he had brought quite a large family here.

Some did not come, preferring the hardships of Europe where their roots had sunk in.

They should have come. Those the Nazis didn't send to the ovens on their way to Russia, the Russians slaughtered on their way to Germany.

That, to my father, was typical of the Gentile (Christian).

I remember him from my boyhood as a quiet, intelligent man with a rapier sense of humor, who used to read the newspaper carefully every day to see how the Jews were making out around the world. He was completely bald, and not impressive physically, but his eyes bored through you. He couldn't be lied to successfully.

His lifelong avoidance of the Gentile was carried out at home and in business. He was coldly courteous to Gentile customers, yet he always dealt fairly. I knew he had a good reputation for bill-paying and equitable business practices. But a Gentile was a Gentile.

I remember the relationship between my father and his mechanic, a Gentile named Matthew. For twenty years that mechanic had repaired my father's cars perfectly. My father paid cash at all times, never using credit for anything. In twenty years neither Matthew nor my father ever smiled while doing business.

When I got a car I naturally took it to Matthew, but he didn't like me. Instead he had his son fix my car. His son was a terrible mechanic, and I always wanted to "pay later." I could imagine Matthew saying to himself, *Here comes Joe Levitt's dumb son to do business with my dumb son.*

Even after I had moved away from Pittsburgh I would bring my car to Matthew for a check-up anytime I came through. One time he said to me, "I haven't seen your dad for awhile."

"He died last winter," I said.

I turned away so Matthew could cry unnoticed.

My father's natural enemy was the Gentile policeman. I'm glad we never had burglars, because my father would die before asking help from the police.

One time the police put up a No Parking sign in front of my father's store. My father ignored the sign and continued to park every day where he always had. It was his land!

The police ticketed the car daily, and my father routinely came out each evening, tore up the ticket with a flourish, and drove home.

Finally, a policeman came to the door at home with a warrant for my father's arrest. He was a tall, pink-cheeked youth in a snappy new uniform, obviously gaining experience in relations with citizens.

He had quite an experience at our house!

My father answered the door. He was about sixty at the time, but was in no way afraid of the strapping young policeman.

Father began the interview. "You get the hell off my property!"

"Sorry, Mr. Levitt. I have a warrant for your arrest. You owe for some parking tickets."

"Didn't you hear me?" my father screamed, lunging at the cop to throw him off the property!

The policeman was astonished. Did this little old man want to fight? He had never encountered a situation like this before.

And he left! Either he wasn't really authorized to take my father away, or he was just plain impressed and yielded to the better man.

The next morning my father parked his car under the No Parking sign and went about his business.

The police made a shrewd move. They sent a Jewish lady who worked at the police station to see my father. She brought records of all the tickets and was prepared to make a settlement. My father bargained with her and managed to get a discount. She accepted the payment, and my father never parked out front again.

He wasn't always angry at things, of course. He had the broad calm of the philosopher who's seen it all.

When I was learning to drive I wrecked his car to the tune of three hundred dollars in damage. He reacted in Yiddish, "Kleine, kinder, kleine tzouris; grosse kinder, grosse tzouris" ("Little kids, little troubles; big kids, big troubles").

One time I was selling on the road during a college summer. I was having a rough time, and he always wanted to check my commissions, since he had sold on the road too. I'd had a terrible week trying to sell to farmers in one instance, but I had been at a rabbit farm and had brought back two little rabbits.

I called my father to give the report.

"How'd you make out this week?" he asked.

"Well, just twenty-seven dollars."

"Twenty-seven dollars! For the whole week?!"

"Yes. But I brought back two rabbits."

"Smart move," he said.

At his funeral the Rabbi made an interesting point. "Who remembers Joe Levitt?" he asked. "We're gathered here to remember a man whom very few are going to remember. Some men die famous; they're called the pillars of the community. Sometimes they help hold up the building and sometimes they're fake—just for looks.

"But there are other pillars inside the walls. They *always* hold up the building. Joe Levitt was one of those inside pillars. Without him, and those like him, our building would fall."

The Rabbi stressed my father's allegiance to the Jewish faith. He was commended for his synagogue attendance, his orderly life, and what we Christians would call "a good testimony."

He had kept the law, kept the faith, and held off the Gentile for seventy years.

And that's a Jew.

Now here's the big question. Which of us Christians would be ready to share "the faith of the Gentile" with my father if he were still alive?

Now that you know something about my father you can imagine how he'd react to Christ, whom he thought of as the Number One Gentile.

A Christian witness would be treated by my father like the policeman at the door! Maybe even worse, because the cop at least had legitimate business to take up with my father. My father wouldn't have considered the Gospel to be legitimate business.

Father would certainly have liked the abundant life in Christ, but he thought of Christianity as the religion of policemen, soldiers, and Jewhaters in general.

And after all, which of us could convict him of sin?

3

Witness to a Jew? Why Bother?

So why bother?

Why not just let my father and all the other hard-headed Jews die in their sins? Haven't we got enough to do for our Lord without getting involved in such an impossible assignment as sharing the faith with Jews?

If they don't appreciate our efforts—our love—our precious Lord—why bother?

Well, we *have* to bother. It's our Lord's commandment. More than that, it's something really special to Him.

God said: "I will bless those who bless you [the Jewish nation]" (Genesis 12:3).

Christ said: " . . . to the extent that you did

it to one of these brothers of Mine, even the least of them, you did it to Me" (Matthew 25:40).

Paul said: "Brethren, my heart's desire and prayer to God for them [Israel] is for their salvation" (Romans 10:1).

The attitude is clear.

The Jews are to be brought to Christ, somehow. This is what God wants.

Furthermore, there is an implication that we must not avoid this commission. God's statement in Genesis goes on to admonish: " . . . and the one who curses you I will curse." Christ is saying with His statement, "Do wrong to them and you do wrong to Me." And if Paul's heart's desire and prayer was to save Israel, who are we to turn away from the task?

It's not easy. But which of our Lord's commandments is easy?

We get certain rewards when we bring the Jew to the faith, as we do whenever we carry out our Lord's plan. They're very practical and very Christian.

The rewards, in simplest form, are (1) a more intimate knowledge of our Lord, (2) a stronger church, and (3) an earlier Second Coming.

The more intimate knowledge of our Lord comes from our gaining insights about the Jewish customs and holidays from the Jew. Our Lord faithfully celebrated the Jewish holidays, as we know. We often say that we want to imitate Christ, but how often do we think about how important the Jewish holidays were for Him?

When we look at Passover, Tabernacles, and the other Jewish festivals in a later chapter we'll see just what meaning these God-given celebrations had for Jesus Christ. Unfortunately, the average Gentile Christian hasn't the vaguest notion of the import of the Last Supper or Tabernacles or Pentecost, etc. As the Gentile Christian goes on celebrating and honoring the Babylonian goddess of fertility, Ishtar (Easter), it must grieve our Lord to see His beloved Passover defamed.

But should the Jew and the Gentile sit down together in consultation about Jesus they would find much to give each other. It's just possible that the Jew, with his almost secret understanding of the ways of God, might well be able to make Jesus more clear to his Gentile brother. And the saved Gentile, with his tremendous gift of discipleship, might well save the Jew and bring him to his true Promised Land, God's Kingdom.

As for the Gentile Christian gaining a stronger church by bringing in his Jewish brethren, there are very logical scriptural and secular reasons.

Scripturally, we find God's ideal church pictured in Ephesians: "For through Him we both [Jews and Gentiles] have our access in one Spirit to the Father ... having been built upon the foundation of the apostles and prophets, Christ Jesus Himself being the cornerstone; in whom the whole building, being fitted together is growing into a holy temple in the Lord" (Ephesians 2: 18,20-21).

Clearly, the Gentile and the Jew belong together in Christ; "For He Himself is our peace, who made both groups into one" (Ephesians 2:14).

Speaking for a moment in a purely practical, secular way, it is easy to see that the Jew and Gentile in Christ make a fine combination. The Jew tends to be earthy, sensitive, steeped in faith ("Trust I got!") by birth and by ancestry. The Gentile is rather practical, efficient, up-to-date. The Gentile usually is a good organizer; the Jew a good businessman.

Few synagogues suffer from lack of membership or lack of support. The Jew is a natural to add to the Christian church. And again, it's God's will.

But the most important reason of all has to do with our Lord's promised Second Coming. Isn't that Second Coming the whole point of Christianity? Don't we pray often with John, "Amen, come Lord Jesus"? (Revelation 22:20)

Yet He said He's not coming until the Jews are ready to receive Him.

In Matthew 23:39 our Lord, standing in the Temple of Jerusalem and addressing a wholly Jewish crowd, said, "I say to you, from now on you shall not see Me until you (Jews) say, 'Blessed is He who comes in the name of the Lord.' "

In Matthew 26:29 the Lord says at the Passover table: " . . . I will not drink of this fruit of the vine from now on until that day when I drink it new with you (Jews) in My Father's Kingdom."

Our Lord, who thought it vital to celebrate Passover, will not even drink the Passover wine again until He can partake of that ceremony with Jews in the Kingdom.

In Peter's magnificent sermon to the Jews in Acts 3 he appeals to them to repent and come to the Lord " . . . that He may send Jesus" (Acts 3:19-20).

The Lord will not return until the Jews welcome Him; He will not partake of His beloved Passover wine until they're ready to join Him in the Kingdom.

Shouldn't we get busy? Shouldn't we share with the Jew?

Of course, but it's almost a Christian tradition to imagine that the Jews had their chance and all of them rejected Christ. Therefore there is no hope for them.

Well, it's certainly hard to support the idea that the whole Jewish populace turned their backs on the Lord. They should have done much better, of course, but it is not accurate to condemn the entire nation.

To begin with, we know from John 1:12 ("As many as received Him . . . ") that some

Jews were saved. Then we learn further in the Gospels that the Jews were of two minds about Him when they assembled. They argued in the Temple about His mission and His character.

Then we have the scenes of real lament at Calvary, where the crowd showed that the official policy of the ruling Pharisees was not necessarily the opinion of the people at large.

In the book of Acts we get some pretty impressive figures. In chapter 2, three thousand Jews are converted to Jesus Christ (2:41). Soon after another five thousand are added (4:4). Those are big numbers; there are only thirteen million Jews alive today. At that rate of conversion, we Christians could bring world Jewry to Christ in a few years.

Then of course we know that a Christian church of importance was established in Jerusalem. That church must have been attended by Jews.

So actually, difficult as Jewish evangelism may seem, it was accomplished handily by our apostles, and in more difficult circumstances. The tradition that all the Jews rejected Christ is inaccurate.

We also need to heed our scriptural admonitions. The Gospel has power to save the Jew *first* (Romans 1:16) and was originally sent to the Jew (Acts 3:26). Our Lord told the grieving Canaanite woman in

Matthew 15:24, "I was sent only to the lost sheep of the house of Israel," and He advised His disciples, "Do not go in the way of the Gentiles . . . but rather go to the lost sheep of the house of Israel" (Matthew 10:5-6).

Naturally, the blessing was extended later to the Gentiles. In this instance of the woman from Canaan, the Lord, as soon as He perceived her faith, healed her daughter.

But it surely is mistaken to suppose the gospel was not meant for the Jews, or that Christ is a "Gentile Messiah."

In John 4:22 the Lord utters a startling statement—"Salvation is from the Jews." Now surely the Christian world would be sadly depopulated if it waited upon today's Jew to bring salvation. The Lord may have been illustrating that the truth would eventually be taken to the world by His Jewish disciples and apostles.

But maybe he meant that the Jews are going to bring salvation in the end times. It is intriguing to speculate what sort of evangelist today's Jew would make. (There are, of course, a number of effective Jewish evangelists active today, and we are going to look at the American Board of Missions to the Jews in later chapters.)

If large numbers of Jews came to Christ in our time I think a great many would be interested in passing on the blessing, and would be extremely effective. The Jew usually is a good salesman with a persuasive, gregarious personality and a rare zeal for the things of God.

Could it yet be literally fulfilled— "Salvation is from the Jews"?

In any case, the Jew deserves to hear the Gospel that was sent to him. And in a very real way he deserves an apology, despite his spiritual aloofness. Christians, at least Christians in name, have cursed the Jew, in spite of God's warnings.

Those well-intentioned "Christian" Crusaders of the twelfth century massacred the Jewish population of the Holy Land in the name of our Lord. In one instance they assembled a huge crowd of Jews in Jerusalem, forced them into a wooden synagogue, and burned it to the ground.

The Spanish Inquisition sought to force "Christianity" upon the Jews. Fifty thousand Jewish people were slaughtered in one three-month period.

The Russian Orthodox Church ran a methodical program of extermination and forced conversion of Jewish communities. Bloody pogroms were formulated and carried out as church projects. Clergy led congregations in such assignments as the sealing off and systematic starvation of entire neighborhoods.

Of course we realize that these miserably misguided brethren of the past could not have made the slightest claim to carrying out any sort of Christian doctrine. By their behavior we can see that they were not related to Christ.

But tell it to the Jew.

The Jew does not separate "Gentile" and "Christian." Even Hitler, with his peerless "final solution to the Jewish problem," is regarded as a "Christian." The Pharoahs, Nebuchadnezzar, Titus and the Romans, the Crusaders, the Inquisitors, the Russians, the Nazis, the Arabs are all so many "Christians" to the Jew.

Maybe that black testimony of the past is one of the best reasons for evangelizing the Jew today. As long as the Jew keeps his image of Christians as persecutors he is next to impossible to reach with the Gospel.

Yet we must make the Lord known among the Jews.

A Jewish leader sums up the present Jewish position this way: We don't need any dialogue with Christians. The best they have to offer they have demonstrated in two thousand years of abuse and persecution."

He's got a point.

And he's not just some crank there among the multitudes. He speaks a typical Jewish opinion. My father would have taken him home to dinner.

We're going to look further into the Jewish resistance with a view to understanding the "adversary." I had the honor of hearing a speech on the topic of Key '73 and other Christian evangelical efforts by the brilliant Marc Tanenbaum, Rabbi, social commentator, scholar, and arch-enemy of Jewish evangelism. He was eloquent and devastating. He laid down the law.

He spoke at the March, 1973, meeting of the Dallas Pastors' Association, and he burned their ears.

That normally sedate organization of "nice" Christian leaders, who avoid controversy in the name of the Lord, found themselves in the middle of a verbal war.

You see, the American Board of Missions to the Jews filled the hall with Hebrew Christians that day. And they brought Dr. Sanford Mills, the equal of Rabbi Tanenbaum as a Jew and a scholar, and the senior field evangelist for the ABMJ.

The meeting occasioned a headline in the *Dallas Times Herald* the next day— "Christians, Jews, Air Tensions."

Rabbi Tanenbaum's thoughts are instructive for all Christians. Here is what he said that day.

4

The Rabbi Lays Down the Law

The setting was the splendid Temple
Emanu-El, a Jewish house of worship in
Dallas. The Pastors' Association had elected
to hear the Rabbi on his own ground.

The original plan for the meeting was to
have the Rabbi lay down the law and then
have responses by local Christian and Jewish
commentators. Professor Schubert Ogden,
of the liberal Perkins Theological Seminary
at Southern Methodist University, and the
hosting Rabbi Jack Bemparod of the Temple, were chosen as the commentators.

Dr. Mills and the Hebrew Christians were
admitted reluctantly at the last minute. The

pastors showed all the enthusiasm of the intellectuals at Athens gathering to hear Paul.

There was a kind of hum in the air as the guests arrived in separate groups. The Hebrew-Christian contingent consisted of a number of young people, missionaries of the Dallas ABMJ chapter, including Head Missionary Dr. Thomas S. McCall and his wife, and of course Dr. and Mrs. Mills.

The religion editors of both Dallas newspapers were present and seemed delighted to find rather controversial topics to report. Normally the meetings of such associations are concerned with quieter issues.

The newswomen interviewed parties of the major "factions" present before the meeting began—the Jews, the pastors, and the Hebrew Christians.

Rabbi Tanenbaum began the formal speeches, addressing himself to broad topics. He opened his remarks, "I want to thank the Dallas Pastors' Association for giving me the opportunity to speak in a Jewish temple."

The Rabbi, noted for his understanding of social issues in general, said that the world is becoming "planetized"—we are actually becoming a "global community" as communications and travel make the world a smaller place.

He said that major religious revivals are

merely a kind of reaction against phenomena of the global community; that Christian communes, Jewish "kibbutzes" and the general spiritual renewal witnessed throughout the world today are an attempt to simplify life back to its "pre-global" style.

This harkening back to simplicity and the smaller living units is a good thing; he called it "a genuine life, an anti-anonymnity." He praised "the yearning for personal fulfillment" evident in the small-unit lifestyle.

The Rabbi also said that he has seen such preferences among unbelievers as well, and he cited the street merchants of New York City who sell handcrafted merchandise of their own manufacture "in order to stamp the items with their own personalities."

Key '73, he continued, does allow Christianity to respond to identity needs. "To the degree the Christian leadership responds to the spiritual needs of the people at large, we Jews encourage it," he said.

He cited the gospel as having the power to "transform" and as being a relevant message for all people today.

"But," he continued (and here's the part I was telling you about), "there are objectionable elements in the way Key '73 is being promoted. The slogan 'Calling the Continent to Christ' is plainly relevant to only a certain interest group."

The Rabbi sketched American religious history and said that Jews and Catholics had suffered a "second-class citizenship" due to evangelical attempts by the larger Protestant church. He gave instances of Jews and Catholics being refused public office, or having to take oaths evangelical in nature in order to serve in government.

Specifically referring to the directions for sharing the Christian faith with the Jews as given in the Key '73 literature, the Rabbi commented, "This is just gauze to get to Jewish defamation." He cited "code words" utilized in the Key '73 publications which are to be substituted for normal Christian vernacular when sharing with Jews. "Messiah" was to be used instead of "Savior," for example, according to the literature.

He said that this approach to Jewish evangelism was defamatory to Judaism, and that "defaming is the theological substructire for antisemitism." He said that the worst results of antisemitism throughout history had theological bases originally.

He particularly cited the American Board of Missions to the Jews for the utilization of "defamatory techniques," and said that the organization had been founded by "those ignorant of Judaism—its wealth of tradition, poetry, literatures, etc."

He claimed that the ABMJ was financially backed by Christian evangelical interests and that the organization had spent one million dollars per convert since its inception.

He also indicted Campus Crusade for Christ, another organization with some outreach to the Jews, for "shill game" techniques. He referred to specific cases, including one in which CCC members disrupted a synagogue service by testifying for Jesus aloud in the congregation. He said that that organization holds "Coke parties" on high school campuses as a method to evangelize unsuspecting Jewish youngsters. He said that the Jewish guests are pressed for a decision for Christ at the social gatherings, and later ostracized if they don't accede.

"However well-intentioned is Key '73, under their umbrella is a dangerous Pandora's Box, including Campus Crusade for Christ, Young Life, InterVarsity, the Jews for Jesus movement, and other such organizations which promote social ostracism and intimidation," he concluded.

"It is impermissible—off-limits—for one religious community to undermine the faith of another. There is no 'One Way,' and that thinking leads to a kind of fascism."

Professor Ogden spoke next, in response. He said that church history did not "reflect the true New Testament sense of 'mission'" but was traditionally coercive. He said that he suspected the motives of evangelical drives in general because "they may be just feeling like they need more influence in society . . . . There's a difference between converting people to Christianity and converting them to God and Christ."

Rabbi Bemparod was next to respond, and said, "I am in perfect agreement on the idea of coercion. In fact, there is a legal issue here; in this country one may worship as he pleases, and there comes a time when evangelism interferes with that right. At such times legal proceedings should be started. An example might be evangelism in the public schools, which is going on.

"If a violinist wants to persuade me that violin music is beautiful," concluded the local Rabbi, "he should play the instrument for me, not beat me over the head with it."

That concluded the first part of the program and the meeting recessed for refreshments. There was to be a question period following a five-minute recap by Rabbi Tanenbaum.

Rabbi Tanenbaum said in his recap, "I only wish that I could communicate to all of you what Judaism really is in terms of its great history and tradition. Those unfamiliar with it should never in any way defame it."

The question period was begun with an invitation to Dr. Mills, the Jewish evangelist, to speak at the microphone.

"I could not agree more concerning the issue of coercion," Dr. Mills said. "I was raised an orthodox Jew, and I know the meaning and fullness of Judaism. And I am a Christian with a realization of the meaning of Christianity.

"As to the founders of the American Board of Missions to the Jews being without this knowledge, the fact is that our founder was a student of the Talmud and an orthodox Rabbi. He had callouses between his fingers because he observed the orthodox practice of sleeping only one hour at a time, with a burning candle between his fingers, while studying the Scriptures.

"As for our Mission spending one million dollars per convert, I don't know where we'd get that kind of money. In my time with the Mission I have seen five hundred baptisms.

"And concerning the Rabbi's concept of the world being planetized, or becoming a global community, I can only say that we should all hope it doesn't really happen. 'One world' would be no place for either a Jew or a Christian. St. Paul says, 'Be ye separated . . . .' "

The floor was opened for questions, but only two were permitted, with no answers given by Rabbi Tanenbaum. The chairman felt that both questions were actually statements of Christian faith, rather than questions addressed to the discussion at hand.

Both of the questions had come from the Hebrew Christian contingent.

The meeting was adjourned rather abruptly, with hands still up for more questions. The chairman closed the meeting saying, "For once we can finish on time. We are adjourned."

Rabbi Tanenbaum, however, maintained his position on the podium and was approached by large numbers of Hebrew Christians as well as by the press.

In answer to the Hebrew Christian questions, which came in a flurry, he cited Romans chapters 9-11, saying that God's covenant with the Jews was beyond recall, so that they didn't need to be evangelized.

He called the Jews for Jesus movement "unimpressive."

"They don't know Judaism, that's all," he said. "I would respect a Talmudic scholar who converted, but not this kind of movement. There is a sense of 'swaggering' about it."

As he left, the Rabbi said, "God bless you all."

Now what's to be done with a man like that?

The average Christian witness, Jew or Gentile, could not hold a candle to him for knowledge of God and the magnificent faith called Judaism. His understanding of the New Testament also is complete—but he just doesn't see Jesus as the Messiah.

If you start a scriptural quote, Tanenbaum will finish it for you—word-for-word King James. If you haul out the Old Testament he'll quote you rabbinical interpretations from all ages, some that you never heard of.

He's a powerful, well-studied, upright lover of God.

And dead in his sins.

Well, believe it or not, that Rabbi can be saved. That little conference at the podium after his speech was for the purpose of witnessing. Those die-hard ABMJ Hebrew Christians were approaching him for the sake of God's love.

And who knows what might have gone on in the Rabbi's heart at the sight of those hopeful Jewish faces all around him, and the power of God's special care for the Jews emanating from them.

Like my father, the Rabbi is a special case. You don't run into that kind of resistance in a heathen. And special cases require special handling.

I was dragged, kicking and screaming, to Christ by Gentiles. The good witnesses of Campus Crusade for Christ were largely responsible for my conversion. I had to admit they had something, even though I didn't like them.

How much simpler it would have been if one of my own people, or at least someone knowledgeable in what a Jew really is, had brought the Gospel to me.

Later I became associated with the American Board of Missions to the Jews and I attended their fellowship meetings. Now that was soothing! There I met my fellow Jews in common worship of Christ.

I don't want to overly praise this one of God's many outreaches to His Chosen People. I am not in the pay of this mission. But in their work I see the solution to the dilemma we've been talking about. The ABMJ educates its missionaries in Judaism until they would be a match for my father or even for Rabbi Tanenbaum. And the mission grants the Jew the respect he deserves in the eyes of God.

In the following section I want to spell out what the mission does, for the purpose of looking at an answer to the various questions we've raised here.

Here's how the Gospel is brought "to the Jew first."

5

"To The Jew First"

If you're a Christian the world hates you; Jesus said it would.

If you're a Jew the world hates you; that's tradition.

The American Board of Missions to the Jews is trying to sell people the idea of becoming Jewish Christians.

It's like the old Jewish joke about the black man reading a Yiddish newspaper. When asked if he's Jewish he sighs, "Das velt mir noch (That I really need)!"

But as we see in the New Testament, it can be done. The ABMJ and other missions to the Jews are bringing the gospel to the

Chosen People with such effectiveness that a very real "Jews for Jesus" movement is an international reality.

There's even a Jews for Jesus movement in Jerusalem. I guess that completes a full circle. After all, it started there.

When you think of it, it's pretty hard to go anywhere in the world and not find Jews. Did God in His infinite wisdom disperse His people so widely in order to ensure His own promulgation? Wherever you find a Jew, God already is known. You can start with step two.

I am not acquainted with every organization that has an outreach to the Jews, but I know the ABMJ very well. I serve as a speaker for one of the local missions, traveling to churches. And I have had occasion to look into how the Mission came to be. I think it's worth a look at the story of one of the local ABMJ missions—that of Los Angeles—to see this "impossible" project in motion.

Los Angeles is the site of ABMJ's training academy for evangelists, and is typical of the "good fight" of Jewish evangelism everywhere. When I visited there I heard the history of the work, and couldn't help but appreciate it as a kind of revolutionary testimony to God's continuing willingness to work miracles.

Here's that story.

"You can't speak in the YMCA building,

and I'll see to it that every church in this city is closed to you!"

That was the typical beginning of God's outreach to the Jews of Los Angeles. The conversation was held on the telephone between Joseph Hoffman Cohen, the first AMBJ missionary, and the manager of the Los Angeles YMCA. It was 1911, near the beginning of Cohen's monumental missionary journeys through the U.S. The speaking date had been arranged by correspondence, but obviously someone had not considered the opinions of the local Christian powers.

Cohen took it philosophically. As he points out in his book *I Have Fought a Good Fight*, "The very claim that I made, that the Gospel must be given 'to the Jew first,' seemed to infuriate some of the very best of the Lord's people in the churches. For so many years they had been taught that the Jew's chance was gone, and here was I, daring to smash down this idol of their doctrinal souls!"

Joseph had one hundred dollars in his pocket and was standing in the midst of Los Angeles "with no place to go," as they say. But God had brought him there to share the faith. What should he do?

We should pause for a definition of the Yiddish term *chootspah* to appreciate the next action of apostle Cohen. *Chootspah* means raw nerve, or audacity, and is ordinarily a complimentary term. We might use it in describing the actions of the apostle Paul when he spoke to the Athenians or when he defended himself in various court-rooms.

Joseph Cohen decided that the auditorium of the great downtown Temple Baptist Church of Los Angeles would be suitable for his message, and made an appointment with the pastor. It was the week before Christmas, an ideal time, Cohen thought, to attract a good turnout.

The pastor just laughed.

It would be impossible for Joseph to have the pulpit, he told the young missionary, and, in any case, Christmas Sunday was pretty well booked up, morning and evening.

"Can you let me have the auditorium for the afternoon?" Cohen asked.

The pastor was exasperated. "Who do you think would come out to hear you—an unknown nobody—on Christmas Sunday afternoon?" But he finally gave in to Cohen's persistence and told the youngster to check the renting office elsewhere in the building. Cohen would have to pay for the hall if he just *had* to speak there.

And that's what Cohen did. He paid the punishingly high rent (for those days) of fifty dollars for two hour's use of the Philharmonic Auditorium, as Temple Baptist Church's plush hall was called. He was provided a backdrop curtain, a table for the stage, and two chairs. And he was accorded the privilege of placing a display easel in the lobby of the auditorium for the rest of that week.

Cohen had a sign lettered and placed it in the lobby next to a poster advertising the appearance of Enrico Caruso of the Metropolitan Opera Company in the same hall. He had ten thousand announcement cards printed up,and went around town placing them in church pews and on parked autos.

It proved to be necessary to stop back at the auditorium now and then and replace the sign on its easel. It kept mysteriously disappearing into closets or behind doors. Cohen patiently searched it out and put it up again beside Caruso's announcement.

"While Caruso could sing better than me, he could not begin to deliver the message that God had given me to deliver," Cohen muses in his memoirs. "So in my heart of hearts I was really better than Caruso."

Cohen would have liked to purchase newspaper space to advertise his unique program, but the expenses of the promotion thus far had run him broke. He literally did not leave himself enough money for his meals.

But he tried the papers anyway, praying they would be interested in his efforts from a church news angle.

His idea worked. One city editor found the whole thing irresistible, and Joseph

Cohen, who insisted the Gospel must be brought to the Jew first, had his picture in the Saturday paper, on the church page.

It was a happy Saturday from that standpoint, but Cohen was getting hungry. After breakfast Saturday he had only one silver dollar to his name, and that had to be saved for a possible emergency telegram back to New York.

He went to bed on an empty stomach Saturday night, hoping he might sleep a long time, since there would be no breakfast or lunch before the program. But he woke up early, spent a nervous morning in earnest prayer, and finally went by the hall at two o'clock, wondering if anyone would show up.

He was bowled over!

The mob which had collected an hour before the program reached out into the street. When the door opened they nearly filled the hall. And more came. And more and more—fifteen hundred in all.

Cohen added to his message the story of his battle to be heard, and how the Lord had opened doors. "I paid fifty good Jewish dollars for this auditorium because I knew the Lord had given me a message and I insisted on being heard, even if it cost me the last ounce of strength I had," he said.

There were no ushers to take up the collection for the mission, so Cohen picked volunteers at random. Derby hats were passed. Afterwards, many people came forward pressing bills into the youthful speaker's pockets and asking him to get in touch with them personally. He was handed dozens of addresses and business cards.

In all, those good Christians gave fourteen hundred dollars to the mission.

Cohen left the hall as soon as possible to have a meal.

Rumors among envious church officials brought this figure to ten thousand dollars. And they had thought they had a great talent when they booked Caruso!

"Well, you just can't beat the Jew," one of them said.

Now that's step one. To bring the Gospel to the Jew first you've got to bring the need for Jewish evangelism to the Christian first.

That's because the (Gentile) Christian seems to own the Gospel these days. He is virtually the sole proprietor of Christ and His gift of salvation. Wouldn't *that* shock Peter!

Joseph Hoffman Cohen's story has been repeated everywhere Jewish evangelism has been attempted, and the successes—considering the odds—have been remarkable. It's apparent to anyone knowledgeable in Jewish evangelism that God is sticking by His promise to Abraham and means to once again rescue His Chosen People.

I remember that before my coming to Jesus I used to laugh at the idea of Christians trying to share their faith with the Jews. *How ridiculous for these neophytes to even approach the true masters of religious faith,* I thought.

But having seen Jewish evangelism in action, and having felt for myself the wonders of new life in Christ, I see it's no laughing matter.

We have looked at the beginnings of a mission to the Jews in this country—how the first step was accomplished. I'd like to go now to the modern picture.

Some people think evangelizing the Jew is just a matter of explaining the Gospel, then standing back to watch the miracle of conversion. But there's more to it than that!

We already have seen that the Jew is a special case, that sharing the faith with my father or Rabbi Tanenbaum requires a creative approach, to say the least.

I was able to sit down with Rev. Harold Sevener, director of the Los Angeles ABMJ installation, and learn something about "the good fight" as it's done today.

I want to share with you the very real dangers and the pure "heart" involved in this work.

6

A Method in Their Matzoh

Rev. Harold Sevener was born to this kind of work. He always had a special burden for the Jews and their salvation.

I don't mean to glorify one man by this, or to say that the Lord is powerless to help the Jews without this kind of available talent, but this particular evangelist exemplifies the personality and training of the missionary to the Jews.

I knew that he was a seminary graduate and had spent some time in the Holy Land. I was impressed with his thorough knowledge of both Testaments, and with his excellent Hebrew and Yiddish.

I was dumbstruck to find out that he was a Gentile.

Oy, did he look Jewish!

Harold attended the American Institute of Holy Land Studies in Israel after his American seminary education, and observed some really sloppy Jewish evangelism in Jerusalem. He refers to the efforts he saw as "the Gentilizing of the Jews."

Can you imagine—worship services were held at 11 A.M. on Sundays, as if that were some sacrosanct hour to the Lord! The Jews couldn't make it if they wanted to—Saturday is the Sabbath in Israel, Sunday a regular workday.

The well-meaning American evangelists held their services in English. Most Israeli Jews don't speak English, and don't have a particular liking for those who do. They'd had their troubles with the soldiers of Great Britain, just as with the soldiers of Rome.

(We must remember that Christ's message is global, not American. We like to think of this country as very Christian, but God's Kingdom is not of this world and doesn't fly any earthly flag.)

The services didn't go unattended; Christians, curious Arabs, and a few students of the English language turned up. But it surely wasn't what you would call a Jewish get-together.

Harold decided to set up the first truly

Hebrew Christian service in Israel since the time of James. He held it on the Sabbath, in the language of the Jews (and Jesus), and he took great care to emulate that special gravity the Jew accords his own worship.

The Jewish response was excellent. An entire kibbutz (Israeli cooperative farm) attended the service.

The service was held at a church, which was not especially appealing to the Jews, but was enhanced by musical recitals—such as renderings of the great works of that fine Christian J.S. Bach. The love of fine music, almost a cultural heritage of the Jews, was thus catered to.

Harold also advocated the celebration of the various Jewish holidays throughout the year, in their full significance in Christ. Passover, Dedication, Tabernacles, and the other Jewish feasts were commemorated by the Christians, just as Jesus commemorated them.

The apostle Paul's statement, "To the Jew I became as a Jew," was adopted by Harold. Then he was "called by the Lord" to the ABMJ and Los Angeles.

Different cities present different evangelical problems, as was true for the early churches of Corinth, Ephesus, and the others. Los Angeles, with its generous mix of peoples and issues, presented some unusual situations.

Take the reaction to the now-famous Passover telecast of the ABMJ.

This succinct presentation of the Jewish Passover feast, with its Christian symbolisms explained, brought five thousand letters of response to the Los Angeles TV station which carried it in 1969. The majority were positive reactions; only three letters were downright hostile, Harold reports.

The national response ran from commentary on the intelligence and scholarship of the presentation to the idea that it was an anti-Semitic sacrilege. *Time* magazine noted the promotional efforts of the ABMJ on the part of the Messiah in an article "A Method in Their Matzoh" (April 1970).

In the Los Angeles area three Rabbis wanted to discuss the validity of the film on the same TV station. The station gave permission, and a great many people tuned in.

As it happened, the discussion went afield of its subject and ended up in an argument over whether the mission had the right to preach the gospel. Two of the Rabbis eventually conceded that in a free country anyone might preach whatever he likes. The third Rabbi, the originator of the discussion, held that the mission was morally wrong to bring Christ to the Jews.

The station manager reported a more favorable response to the moderate view. The third Rabbi was considered too harsh.

At the L.A. mission that year, Hebrew Christian Passover tickets went like hotcakes (unleavened).

So many people wanted to attend, the Mission had to find extra space. One of the workers set out to rent a synagogue building. In his search he found one available.

It was the synagogue of that particularly objecting third Rabbi in the TV debate.

Harold assumed that this was just good humor on the part of the Lord and went ahead with the arrangements. Eventually the Rabbi found out.

"What *chootzpah!*" he exclaimed, and canceled the program. The ABMJ made other arrangements in time.

But the Rabbi wasn't finished with his protests. He brought a busload of young people from his congregation and picketed the ABMJ Passover services!

The youngsters carried posters in front of the hall as other people went in. One read, "Thou shalt not covet thy neighbor's soul." Harold called the newspapers and asked for coverage of the unique event. As in the case of Joseph Cohen, the press could see the news value inherent in Jewish evangelism. They came in force.

Harold talked to the picketers, to try to bring them to Christ. At first they seemed to regard him as some kind of demon making war on their valued ancient traditions. But little by little they began to respond. They had been briefed on what to say to the Hebrew Christian evangelists. And the Rabbi, with true appreciation for the potency of the gospel, had charged his picketers to speak to the Christians only in groups of two.

"Don't let those Christians get you alone," he had warned.

Harold offered to carry one boy's sign while the youngster went inside to the services.

"What do you say?" Harold asked.

"I don't know what to say," the boy replied. "That wasn't in our script!"

Somehow the Christians got the pickets to go into the services in small groups. There they saw the familiar Passover tables and heard a few new things. Some of them learned for the first time that Christ Himself celebrated the Passover, on His last earthly day.

Some learned that Christ is Jewish.

And maybe one or two realized that He was the Messiah.

That kind of event is the daily bread of the AMBJ. With the apostle Paul, they can truly say they "fight" for Christ.

Unfortunately this becomes literal when club-swinging Jewish Defense League members take exception to the evangelism. Threats allegedly have been made on the lives of the Hebrew Christian evangelists of Los Angeles and their families. The ABMJ prays for these misguided brethren who so zealously defend their faith.

The stories of battle for Christ—of Rabbis pitted against missionaries and synagogues against missions—make the headlines of Jewish evangelism. But the behind-the-scenes work—the discipling of the Jews one by one—is the real stuff of this part of God's calling. Here Harold has a few memories he calls "precious."

There was the old Jewish gentleman with the thick Viennese accent who turned up for one of the weekly devotional services. The services are not meant to be formal, like those at big churches, but only to honor the Jew and his Messiah. There usually is Bible study, a short sermonette and refreshments. No special Christian artifacts are on display. The fellowship is warm and informal.

The Viennese gentleman was polite and attentive. He was a patient man. His body bore the scars of his years in the concentration camps.

He returned week in and week out and was appreciated as a quietly learned man with an open mind. No one approached him directly with the gospel, although all prayed for his salvation.

Finally one evening he said to the head missionary, "I really should read the New Testament and do some thinking about it. I'm not going to come back for awhile, but I promise you that I will consider what you've said here. Should I return, I'll gladly become one of you. I'll believe in Christ."

And he did return; he did receive his Messiah.

Five years later!

Then there was the retired bank vice-president. He was sharp. He'd spent forty years behind his desk in a big bank listening to people trying to fool him. He almost knew what you were thinking before you said it.

Probably his interest in Judaism wasn't all that strong, but he was a shrewd man. He wasn't going to make any change unless it paid him dividends. He was a banker, not a speculator.

But he enjoyed good fellowship no matter what it was based on. He came regularly to the mission services for the general good cheer. He was old and widowed and didn't have much company. Although he tended to be a bit crabby, he seemed to appreciate people reaching out.

He told the mission people one night that he was thinking about becoming a Christian, but he had to talk it over with his wife.

He did. He went to the cemetery, stood at his wife's grave and talked it over with her. He made many trips, over a period of months, until he ascertained that his wife—his one true friend—had no objections.

Then he received Christ. He's an active and loving Christian today.

Harold was personally involved in the salvation of Isadore Roth, synagogue president and Orthodox Jew without peer. The aged Mr. Roth was the very picture of the fine old Jew, bent in prayer and supplication, who represents to the Western World its roots of faith in one God.

We've all known this kind of man—whether Jew or of some other faith. There is an intense passion in his way of doing things, and we can't fault him because we ourselves are mere shadows of his kind of accomplishment.

Mr. Roth knew God as we think of Abraham knowing God. His testimony was excellent. He despised no one, because the Old Testament teaches, "Love thy neighbor." He was looked up to as only a humble man can be.

He believed absolutely and implicitly in the Law of Moses, and he carried out to the letter every one of the complex traditions of Orthodox Jewry every day of his life.

Isadore Roth would smile in pity at the Campus Crusader who says, "Your Judaism isn't good enough for salvation, don't you see? The law never saved anyone."

His deeply felt faith and his knowledge of the essence of Judaism were respected far and wide. Rabbis sought his opinions. The Christian clergy were pleased to receive him. He was a fine, respectable man, honored in his community by Jew and Gentile alike.

When Harold met him he was dying.

But Mr. Roth was not dying the death of one of the Chosen People whose God has accepted his atonement. Mr. Roth was confused. He was not ready to die.

It was a subtle thing. Harold was overwhelmed by the profound emotions of this patriarch, decades his senior in the worship of God the Father, who was dying in spiritual discomfort.

The High Holidays had just passed. Mr. Roth had observed the Ten Awesome Days between the Rosh Hashanah and the Yom Kippur, in which he might repent before God. He had fasted, despite his mortal illness, on Yom Kippur—the Day of Atonement—and he had asked God to be inscribed in the Book of Life, as he had done yearly throughout his long life of service.

But this time he did not feel forgiven. He knew he was dying. But there was a way to die, and a way not to die.

From his bed he told Harold in a trembling voice, "I thought I had confessed everything, but . . . ."

With all of the earnestness and all of the respect he could muster, Harold began to share the faith.

"Your atonement before God has been

done. The Messiah has done it for you. Your sins are forgiven . . . ."

Sometime later Mr. Roth told his friends, "I believe in Yeshuah (Jesus). I have found peace." He was smiling and content.

Soon after, he died.

In any kind of evangelism it's those "war stories"—the head-to-head confrontations over the gospel—that really tell the story. And somehow when the Jew is involved the story has a special meaning.

In Los Angeles, and the other cities where the mission holds it unique worship services, many Jews gather along with their Gentile brethren to honor the Messiah. The Gentiles were there already; the Jews were brought, one by one like Isadore Roth, to the faith.

7

Passover and Other Christian Rites

So goes the battle of Los Angeles.

But personally, in my own ministry I'm more familiar with the battle of, say, Hillsdale, Oklahoma, population seventy souls.

It's a tiny speck in the midst of the vast wheat fields of the southwestern plain, but though it be little among the thousands, Christ is well-known there as a Jew.

The Congregational Church of Hillsdale flies me in every few months to remind them that Jesus is Jewish.

I hold Passover with them. I put on my *kittel,* the white ceremonial Passover robe, and my *yarmulke*, the festival prayer crown, and I impart to them the following:

1. The Passover Plot

Are the great Jewish festivals, still faithfully commemorated year in and year out since the time of Moses, just pagan rituals?

Has God had second thoughts about His pronouncements in the book of Leviticus, wherein He gave exact directions as to the celebration of Passover and the other feasts?

As a matter of fact, the very existence of these festivals is a fascinating proof of the timelessness of God, and the way He sees forward to eternity at a glance.

The feasts are more than "Jewish" or "Christian."

For men they are a picture of world history from Christ to Christ—from His birth to His coming Kingdom.

For God they are a diagram of His creation; a working model of His plan from chaos to eternity.

Let's look at His model, beginning with Passover.

It is astonishing to Jews and Christians alike that Passover, the crown jewel of Jewish festivals, tells the story of Christ in its symbols.

The feast is meant to recount the great exodus of God's people from their slavery in Egypt, but God in His subtlety has woven the life and times of the Messiah into the ceremony.

Take the lighting of the candles at the beginning of the feast. A woman must light the candles and make the blessing which thanks God for the Light. Judaism otherwise is certainly no feminine religion, and in the orthodox synagogue the women cannot even sit in the company of the men, let alone pronounce prayers. Yet a woman must bring the light to the Passover table.

And this is the point—God chose a woman to bring forth the Light of the world, the Messiah.

Christ might well have appeared on the earth in the manner of God appearing to Moses—straight from heaven—but God elected to have His Son "born of woman." In John 8:12 Christ verifies that He is "the Light of the world."

Then there's the idea of ceremoniously cleaning out the leaven from the house before it is properly sanctified for Passover. Leaven, or yeast, is the ingredient of bread that makes it rise. The flat matzohs eaten by the Jews on Passover—the same as eaten by the Lord at the Last Supper—contain no leaven. Leaven is symbolic of sin (I Corinthians 5:6-8). The Lord was "unleavened"; the apostle Paul refers to Him as "Christ, our Passover" in I Corinthians 5:7. The Jewish home is, in effect, made suitable for the honoring of Christ at Passover.

The "blood of the Lamb" is remembered on Passover by the Jews. They refer to the blood of sacrificial lambs which was used to mark their doorposts in Egypt so that the angel would *pass over* the Jewish homes, while slaying the first-born son in the Egyptian dwellings.

To the Christian the blood of the Lamb has exactly the same meaning; Christ's blood redeems us, and spares us God's judgment (John 1:29). Judaism and Christianity coincide on this symbol.

The ceremonial plate on the Passover table bears the shankbone of a lamb. This recalls for the Jew the happier times when the Temple stood and a lamb, God's preferred sacrifice, was eaten at Passover. Its Christian meaning is obvious.

Back to the matzoh—the unleavened bread. Christ identified it as His body. Paul quotes Him, "This is My body, broken for you" (I Corinthians 11:24).

As part of the Passover ceremony the father of the house solemnly breaks a piece of matzoh!

Take a piece of matzoh and look at it carefully. Does it really symbolize the Lord's body?

It is unleavened. It has stripes ("By His stripes we are healed"—Isaiah 53:5). And it is pierced ("They will look upon Him Whom they have pierced . . ."—Zechariah 12:10). It has actual holes.

The matzoh always turns out this way because of the way it is prepared. How astute it was of our Lord to choose so apt a symbol.

More important than the appearance of the matzoh is what is done with it as part of the Passover ceremonies. Three pieces of matzoh are involved; it is the middle one (the Son, in the Trinity) which is broken.

The broken piece is wrapped in white linen and hidden away (as also was our Lord's body.) It is brought forth again to the table during the *third* cup of wine.

Convincing? Symbolic of the resurrection?

The clincher is the ceremonial name of the third cup. It is called "the cup of redemption."

Finally at the conclusion of the ceremony, Elijah's cup is brought forward. A place has been set at the table for Elijah, the prophet who is to come to announce the Messiah, and an empty cup awaits his honored presence.

A child is sent to open the door of the house in case Elijah arrives with his long-awaited good news.

It is heartbreaking to think of the Jew awaiting Elijah through the millennia and setting out his cup on every Passover in every home, particularly when we consider that the Lord clearly identified John the Baptist as Elijah.

Elijah already has come. His job has been done. He has announced the Messiah. He said of Christ, "Behold the Lamb of God!" an unmistakable identification for the Jewish onlookers.

This ceremony comes last in the Jewish feast because the Jew believes the Messiah is yet to arrive.

Our prayer is not to discontinue Passover, which our Lord loved, but to place the cup of Elijah where it belongs in the magnificent celebration—between the lighting of the candles and the burial of the unleavened bread (between our Lord's birth and His earthly death).

We owe it to John the Baptist, Elijah in the flesh.

2. God's Calendar

All of the other Jewish festivals celebrate Christ and the other outworkings of God's plan. They are a constant reminder that in the mind of God there is no difference between Christianity and Judaism, as long as the Messiah is honored.

A Jew accepting Christ is a perfect Christian. A Christian is a perfect Jew.

We must realize that the seven Jewish festivals announced in the Old Testament, and carried out since that time, are not man-made ceremonies. They are a part of God's Word, given by Him. The schedule of annual events is given in Leviticus 23.

The Jewish year is "God's Calendar."

It begins with Passover, in Nisan, the first Jewish month (Leviticus 23:5). This falls in March and April on our modern calendar. Passover, as we have seen, commemorates the death of the Sacrificial Lamb.

The day following the Passover feast starts the week of unleavened bread (Leviticus 23:6). This represents a communion with Christ— a holy, "unleavened" walk.

So the Passover period represents first the sacrifice (redemption) and then fellowship with Christ (the holy walk).

But there is still a third ceremony in the Passover period. The Feast of the First Fruits is celebrated on Sunday ("on the morrow after the Sabbath") during this festival period (Leviticus 23:10-12).

"First Fruits" looks prophetically to the time of the Christian being raised. Christ, of course, was the first to be raised in His resurrection body, and God identifies His Son as the "First Fruit" in I Corinthians 15:23.

Then God directs His people to pass fifty days until the fourth feast, the Harvest (Leviticus 23:15,16,21). This is Pentecost, or *shevuous* in Hebrew, and comes in May or June. It marks the coming of the Holy Spirit in the New Testament. The Lord's harvest was great at that first Pentecost after Christ's resurrection: three thousand Jews were saved at that electrifying scene (Acts 2) and another five thousand just afterwards (Acts

4). And the tremendous harvest to come, when Christ takes His Church, is represented on our futuristic calendar by this fourth Feast among the Jewish holidays.

Next in God's plan should come the rapture of the Church to heaven and the regathering of Israel to their Land—and so it does. God next orders the exciting Feast of Trumpets in August-September (Leviticus 23:23). With the "sound of the trumpet" God will gather believers in Christ to heaven (I Thessalonians 4:16-17) and the Jewish people back to Israel (Isaiah 27:13). The Jews sound the trumpet, actually a ram's horn called the *shofar,* in every synagogue on Rosh Hashanah, the Feast of Trumpets.

Only ten days are to pass before the next feast, the sacred Day of Atonement, or Yom Kippur (Leviticus 23:27-29). This is a serious and sanctified day to the Jew, involving fasting and deep repentance. On this day, the Jew prays to be inscribed in the Book of Life for the coming year.

The Jew has much to fear. God says in no uncertain terms in Leviticus 23:29 that "If there is any person who will not humble himself on this same day, he shall be cut off from his people." This is a terrible fate for anybody, but has special menace to the Jew.

The Day of Atonement obviously foresees the judgment of Israel and its redemption. God's symbolism is masterful. He promised to save a remnant of His people, and on that final Yom Kippur He will redeem His promise. When Christ returns to Jerusalem all Israel will be saved (Romans 11:26-27; Zechariah 12:10).

What is left in God's plan for the earth except the millennial kingdom?

Sure enough, the final Jewish festival of the year foresees that idyllic period. Succoth, the Feast of Tabernacles—for which our Lord made that arduous and dangerous journey in John 7—beautifully portrays the millenium, when each man will live peacefully in his own tabernacle, and all will go to Jerusalem to commemorate the feast each year (Leviticus 23:34, Zechariah 14:16-19).

(Gentile Christians often don't realize that these Jewish holidays are going to survive the rapture, Armageddon, the second coming, and everything else. The Lord will celebrate Passover, as was His preference, and we will do it along with Him. Likewise with Tabernacles and the others. The Gentile Christian will have to someday, somehow, learn about these feasts.)

Here's a quick rundown on the Jewish feasts with their Christian symbols. Note the chronological order of God's model:

Date	Jewish Feast	Christian Symbol
March-April	Passover	The Blood
March-April	Unleavened Bread	The Body
March-April	First Fruits	The Resurrection
May-June	The Harvest	Pentecost
August-September	Trumpets	The Rapture
August-September	Atonement	Redemption
August-September	Tabernacles	The Millennium

Note also that there are seven feasts, with the seventh being a time of rest (the Millenium). This symbolized God's earthly week.

It's important to realize that Jews (but not Christians) are continuing to celebrate these feasts, which portray the whole of God's plan for the earth. It suggests that God certainly meant for His Chosen People to participate in His ultimately happy ending for the world. It suggests that the Jew has some information for the Christian.

But since this true appreciation of Christ's role in the feasts has been imparted to Christains, it remains up to Christians to share it with Jews. This is surely God's will.

The people of Hillsdale are spellbound by that message. And they're not the only ones. Gentile Christians everywhere are enthralled by their Jewish heritage and greatly inspired to see God's whole plan in action.

But how does all this help bring Jews to a saving knowledge of their Messiah Jesus Christ?

Well, first, if a Jew ever came through Hillsdale (not likely) he'd be swarmed with the most knowledgeable Christian witnesses he's ever tried to beat off with a stick. They would set him a Passover table that would be the envy of his Old World grandfather. And most important, they would respect him for what he is: a chosen person of God.

It's not likely that Jews would ever be persecuted by anybody from Hillsdale, and that's a step in the right direction. Persecution as a way of conversion has been tried, as we have seen. It doesn't work.

I speak in many churches, conservative and liberal, victorious and lost, rich and poor. I chose Hillsdale here because it's one of the best churches I've seen with respect to worshiping God. There surely is a variety of Christian churches in the U.S.

I've been turned away from churches of all denominations because I am Jewish. To some folks, Jews just aren't kosher. "You want to speak on what? Passover? This is a Christian church, my friend! I'm afraid we can't accommodate you."

But on the whole it's no secret anymore that Jews are okay in church. And nothing will help more in saving the Jew.

In these final two chapters I want to address my Christian and Jewish brothers, respectively. First, I have some suggestions on witnessing to the Jews for Christians, from my own experience and from established sources. Then I have a few things to say to my own brethren, the lost sheep of Israel.

I think we understand the problems. Here, God willing, are some solutions.

8

If It Weren't for Christ
I Wouldn't Be a Christian

I notice my brothers in Christ get a great deal out of their lives of service. They love the churches, the Christian society, the good works, and the missionary outreach for Christ. I love these things, too.

But if that's all there is to Christianity they could keep it.

I love my Lord, and what He and I have together.

The other stuff I had plenty of as a Jew. Believe me, a direct comparison between the Christian life and the Jewish life doesn't show the Jew anything. He does not see any advantage whatsoever to "behaving like a Christian."

But only a fool would reject Jesus Christ if he knew Him, and the Jew is no fool.

This is not to underrate the Christian way of life, but to emphasize Christ. I think He can get forgotten, and that is deadly to any kind of evangelism—and to Jewish evangelism in particular.

Let's look at it this way. When the Christian faith is taken to the jungles and given to the heathen, he hears about God for the first time. His mind is open because he is receiving entirely new and unique information. The Christian life is something new.

Likewise with the heathen of civilization. If a man has never been to church, never participated in helping orphans or feeding the destitute, and never been really loved in his community, he is apt to find the Christian life deeply gratifying. When he comes to Christ, the life itself is rejuvenating.

But the Jew is no heathen. He has his church, his orphanages, his good works. He is loved by his brethren in his community. He lacks none of these things.

He even has a country now, and no longer can be called "the man without a country."

So what does the Jew lack? What do you offer him that he doesn't already have?

The answer of course is Jesus Christ, the Messiah.

The Jew *knows* he needs his Messiah. That is scriptural to the Jew.

If you show the Jew that Christ is his Messiah you don't have to say anything else.

But standing squarely between the Jew and Christ is Christianity as practiced. That includes some real turnoffs for the Jew.

Take prejudice.

If it weren't for the blacks I suppose the Jews could claim a corner on the world market for prejudice. From the beginning of history the Jew has been everybody's scapegoat and the Christian church is no exception.

And I wonder if any kind of prejudice could be more obnoxious to God.

Certainly it wouldn't be fair to accuse all Christians of hating all Jews, but most of us have seen those paranoid little pamphlets that claim that the Jew is a Christ-killer, a pagan, a hater of God, etc.

I had some trouble with a character who said that it was unscriptural for a Christian Gentile to marry a Christian Jew. (Can you imagine our Lord making such distinctions?) This man was a minister and Bible teacher, and he quoted Nehemiah and other sources as commanding the Jew to marry only another Jew.

Of course the Scriptures command the Jew not to marry an idol worshiper, but this wouldn't apply to the case of two Christians. "There is neither Jew nor Greek" in Christ, says the apostle Paul.

I asked my friend if it wasn't just a case of him being a tad prejudiced about the Jews, but he said, "I know God's commandments. I love the Jew!"

Well, love like that the Jew can't live on.

Another friend settled the argument nicely with his comment, "The whole church is going to marry a Jew!"

Some people, even some seminaries, try to disenfranchise the Jewish people of their "chosen" status with God. One line of reasoning goes, "Today's Jews are not the real descendants of the Old Testament Jews—they've descended from forced conversions in the Middle Ages."

What a yarn that is! The Jews do not convert anybody. There is no such procedure scripturally. You cannot become one of the Chosen People—that status is given only by birth. There are no missionary efforts in Judaism at all. (Some synagogues have adopted a conversion procedure similar to the Catholic "Instruction," but this is not scriptural.)

To add a little odor to that conversion story it is sometimes said that those forced conversions to Judaism were made in Russia. That way the Jews come out communist as well as Gentile.

And for a finishing touch there is the Jewish dark complexion—the Jew must have gotten that way intermarrying with Africans. Jews must be partly black!

Those stories are not so fanciful as they may sound here. They are serious, if pathetic, efforts to keep the Jew out of the Christian church, and although they are perpetrated by a minority they don't sit so well with the Jew. And anyway, who says God doesn't love Gentiles, blacks, and communists?

All that is just an introduction to my first suggestion in witnessing to the Jews, and it is simply this: Treat the Jew like a normal person who needs to be saved.

I'm often called on to assist at the weird ceremony known as "witnessing to a Jew." It is thought that my "Jewishness" will overwhelm the lost one.

Well, frankly, although I know a few tricks to the trade I just keep in mind that I'm talking to an individual in need of salvation, like I once was, and I stick to telling him it's available.

I have said many times that the Jew is a special case, and he is. But it serves no good purpose to treat him like a visitor from outer space.

Try treating him as you'd like him to treat you—that was the Lord's recommendation.

But in any case, for heaven's sake, get your prejudices confessed and taken care of before you approach a Jew!

Okay, I think the point is made. Assuming that you are able to regard the Jew as a neutral case, let me go on to practical suggestions for witnessing.

First, it's probably best to avoid discussions of current Jewish and Christian social thinking when witnessing to Jews. When discussing matters of such gravity as the gospel and salvation, social customs and the myriad issues of modern times are trivial. It is not possible to persuade the Jew that the Christian has a better life style, a more loving society, or a better house of worship.

Certainly cultural differences are obvious among peoples of all kinds. God is no respecter of persons; neither is the truly committed Christian. But many witnesses make the mistake of comparing modern trends and trying to convince the Jew that the Christian is "more godly."

The Jew is in fact repelled by the austere attitudes of some Christians; he sees no sense to conservativism of dress and social mannerisms in general. This is just not his way of doing things.

Until we know that God highly values the peculiar manners and styles of current Christianity, we might as well stick to the Gospel.

Some of the Christian worship terminology—"born again," "the blood," "Trinity" and "salvation," to mention a few—have a negative connotation to the Jews. The term "conversion" probably puts off more Jews than any other single word, for obvious reasons.

Stay away from Jewish jokes. To the Jew

they are his possession. Few non-Jews can do a good job of telling them anyway.

Now we come to the difficult manner of love.

All Christians worthy of the name aspire to love one another and all men. But like the saying goes, "They've got a funny way of showing it."

God's children are like anybody's children—those who have been hurt need special portions of love.

The Jew doesn't understand love as a theory; he wants to see it in action.

If you go into a Jewish community so that you really get to know the people, you'll see love in action. It's not the miraculous love given the Christian by the Lord; rather it's arrived at by the camaraderie and spirit of the underdog. It's a result of the efforts of men.

As a Hebrew Christian I have felt the love of both kinds, and I know that love in Christ is superior to that given in the power of men. A loving Christian just can't be beat. But like any Jew, I had to see it in action. I wasn't interested in a "Buyer Protection Plan" when I received Christ; I wanted a good performance right out of the showroom.

Show the Jew, as well as your Christian neighbor, that God is Love.

It is also recommended that the Christian know something about Judaism to converse with the Jew. When young Christians first shared their faith with me, one of them said,

"The Jews are not a nation; they're a race."

I later found this inexplicable and mildly insulting statement printed in some of their literature. Somehow it gave me that old feeling of being some kind of freakish specimen for their lab tests.

Naturally the youngster didn't intend any offense, but it was clear to me that he failed to understand what being a Jew meant.

(We might say in passing that the Jew is the worst possible target for "one-shot evangelism.")

Being up-to-date on what's happening in Israel would make the average Christian an infinitely better witness to the Jews, and is certainly in line with Christian thought about prophecy.

Prayer is something a Jew respects and understands completely. You will probably find a positive reaction when you offer to pray for a Jew. But don't say, "I'll pray for your salvation." Just pray for him. God knows what he needs.

I brought a Jew to Christ once by telling him, "I don't feel as though I have the knowledge to help you with your problems, but if you have no objection I'll ask Christ for guidance." The Lord gave the guidance, and the soul was won.

Praying *with* a Jew brings up another whole problem. Jews pray differently, albeit to the same Source. The idea of praying together is generally best left alone.

If you take a Jew to your church make sure he understands that the church is not the whole of Christianity. If it gets on a level where he compares the synagogue with the church, as reflecting one faith against another, he's going to opt for the synagogue.

And don't fear going to a synagogue. You'll be welcome.

If you do bring your Jewish friend to church, make sure people don't pounce on him like salesmen to bring him to the Lord. It's that "lab specimen" feeling again.

A Hebrew Christian mission is the best place to take a Jew. If the ABMJ has a mission in your area, your guest will be among sensitive specialists in the problem. The other Jewish evangelism organizations are effective, too, and many churches have a good Jewish outreach program featuring a social open house now and then.

Tracts aimed at the Jew can be effective. These are available from the the various Jewish evangelical organizations. Sometimes they are available in Hebrew and Yiddish.

It should be said, though, that the whole area of church, tracts, and modern Christianity in general opens a Pandora's Box of little troubles. There is a constant danger of implying that present-day Christianity is the perfection of Christ's message, whereas we know that we all fall short of it. If the Jew is made to think that church worship, conservative mannerisms, New Testament studies, missionary work, and the other peculiarities of Christianity today reflect the Lord in all His glory, the Jew will turn his back.

The Lord Himself—His love, His power, and His Messiahship—must be stressed if the Jew is to be saved.

If it weren't for Christ I wouldn't be a Christian.

9

For Jews Only

Brethren, there's been a kidnapping!
Our Messiah has been stolen!

Not really "stolen." Appropriated. But not without His knowledge and blessing. When the leaders of our ancestors officially rejected Him, He extended His love and His infinite power to the godless Gentiles. God's most magnificent gift to His Chosen People has been made into some kind of Gentile before our eyes, and it is we who are without God's provision for salvation.

Our Father hears us today. He always has. When we rejected His commandments, when we stoned His prophets, He always was faithful to redeem us. We were punished, but He did not forsake us.

But this time we have rejected His Son.

Still, He waits as always to redeem us.

If you scoff at this you are scoffing at our Testament, our *Tenach.* You are opposing Moses, David, Isaiah, Daniel, Zechariah, Micah, and a host of our other hallowed patriarchs through whom our God gave us the Scriptures.

Never mind the so-called New Testament. Take up your Bible now—*our* Testament, which the *goyim* call the Old Testament—and let us look open-mindedly at the Word of God.

I'm going to assume with you for the moment that the New Testament was a cunning masterpiece of literary engineering that those writers forced to conform to our Bible in order to make Jesus Christ appear to be the Messiah.

And I'm going to say that *our* Bible *still* shows Christ as the One we've always waited for.

Open your Bible to Daniel 9:25. There our honored ancestor Daniel gives his marvelous Seventy Weeks of Years prophecy. He predicts in this verse the time of the coming of the Messiah (and he calls Him "The Messiah," *Mashiach* in Hebrew.)

He says plainly that from the issuing of the decree to rebuild Jerusalem until the arrival of the Messiah would be seven weeks, and threescore and two weeks.

Daniel's "weeks" *(shevuonim)* actually are years. The Hebrew term refers to "sets of seven."

That wonderful decree to rebuild our holy city, and the Temple with it, was given by the benevolent King Artaxerxes in the twentieth year of his reign. This is told in Nehemiah 2:1 and the ensuing portion.

We know from secular sources that Artaxerxes reigned in the fifth century B.C., from 465 to 425. The decree then, according to our Scriptures, was issued in 445 B.C.

Daniel's prophecy was made while he was captive of the Babylonians in the sixth century B.C., so the very issuing of the decree showed his reliability as a prophet.

But let's go on to his prediction about the coming of the Messiah.

We have to calculate "seven weeks, plus threescore and two weeks," which equals sixty-nine weeks, after 445 B.C. The sixty-nine weeks in terms of years add up to 483 years (69x7 years).

We can see that the period Daniel prophesies occurs in the fourth decade of the first century A.D., just the time we know Jesus walked the earth and was crucified.

(A complete arithmetical working out of this prophecy may be found in Sir Robert Anderson's *The Coming Prince.* It shows that Daniel was accurate to the *exact day* of Jesus' triumphal coming into Jerusalem. Or see my book, written with Dr. Thomas S. McCall, *Satan in the Sanctuary,* for the exact figures.)

The prophecy is unassailable. The Jews of antiquity discussed it, so it could not have been interpolated after the events. The very years of King Artaxerxes' reign were not known until modern research uncovered these ancient periods.

It does not surprise us as Jews that Daniel could see the future. But shouldn't we listen to everything he said?

He told us the time of the coming of the Messiah. It's there in your Bible.

This prophecy so persuaded Rabbi Leopold Cohen (the father of Joseph Cohen, the Los Angeles pioneer) a century ago that he went on to receive the Messiah and to found the American Board of Missions to the Jews.

An argument against Jesus being the promised Messiah says that the Messiah was supposed to bring immediate peace and an immediate kingdom. That is a traditional belief, but not a scriptural one.

Look at Isaiah 53. It describes the Messiah suffering on behalf of His people: "He was pierced through for our transgressions, He was crushed for our iniquities . . . He Himself bore the sin of many, and interceded for the transgressors" (Isaiah 53:5,12).

This is surely a different picture of our Messiah than tradition gives us. Yet it is directly from *our* Scriptures.

Zechariah predicts, "They shall look upon Him whom they have pierced" (12:10). Micah foresees, "With a rod they will smite the judge of Israel on the cheek" (5:1). King David laments the very crucifixion of the Messiah, "... they pierced my hands and my feet. I can count all my bones. They look, they stare at me ..." (Psalm 22:16,17).

Obviously the Messiah was to have a bad time of it when He came. King David calls Him "the stone which the builders rejected" (Psalm 118:22).

But why the traditional belief that the Messiah is to triumph?

Well, this idea is in the Scriptures, too. Isaiah's magnificent "For a child will be born to us ..." (9:6,7) foresees the triumph of the Messiah. King David certifies that all kings shall fall down before Him and all nations shall serve Him (Psalm 72:11).

How can one Messiah satisfy both concepts? Is He to suffer or is He to reign supreme?

All Scripture is accurate. It is the gift of God to us, His chosen. The answer is simple: The Messiah comes twice. This is not a Gentile concept. Notice that we have not quoted the so-called New Testament. Our own prophets revealed the first coming, with its rejection and crucifixion, and the second coming, with its complete triumph.

This is not meant to be a complete lesson in Scripture, but only a glance at the more obvious prophecies about our Messiah. Know that there are some three hundred references to Jesus Christ in our Scriptures.

It is established in our Bible that He was to be born in Bethlehem (Micah 5:2) of a virgin (Isaiah 7:14), and would be a prophet of the skill of Moses (Deuteronomy 18:15-19). He was to ride into Jerusalem on a donkey (Zechariah 9:9), be rejected by His own people (Isaiah 53:1-3), and be betrayed by one of His own followers (Psalm 41:9). He was to be tried and condemned (Isaiah 53:8) but to remain silent before His accusers (Isaiah 53:7). He was to be actually spat upon (Isaiah 50:6), mocked (Psalm 22:7,8) and crucified (Psalm 22:14-17).

But His suffering was for a divine purpose; He was to bear it in our place (Isaiah 53:5-12).

Though He was to be tormented with vinegar and gall in His agony (Psalm 69:21) and to see His pitiful garments divided among His torturers by lots (Psalm 22:18), He was to be spared broken bones (Numbers 9:12, Exodus 12:46).

But, praise God, He was to rise from the dead (Psalm 16:10) and sit at the right hand of God Himself (Psalm 110:1).

And at the right time He is to return (Daniel 7:13,14), sit on the throne of David

(Isaiah 9:6,7), and reign over all the earth (Psalm 72:8,11).

Now that is *our* Scripture. If you reject Jesus Christ, at least accept our own prophets and understand that the Messiah has come, been rejected, and will return in triumph.

And if you can be open-minded enough to read the New Testament—even just as literature—do so and see if Jesus fulfills the complex requirements to be the Jewish Messiah.

The only other possibility is that the unlettered authors of the New Testament—that group of Jewish fishermen, tradesmen, and tax collectors—accomplished the fantastic task of forcing the story of Christ to fit the Old Testament.

They would have had to be steeped in the knowledge of the time-honored Old Testament prophecies and traditions, and they would have had to create a conspiracy against their own people. (It is notable that they died martyrs' deaths defending their reports of the Messiah; hardly the behavior of mere inventors.)

Assuming that Jesus is our Messiah, look what's become of Him. The *goyim* have taken Him for their own, which is well and good; who can deny anyone the blessing of communion with God?

But they have "converted" the Messiah!

That's strange, but clearly, Christ has become a "Gentile" with the passing of time. So few Jews have accepted the Messiah that He has come to be regarded as a non-Jew—a perfectly crazy idea.

Our Messiah never gave up His Jewish faith. (Remember that He celebrated the Passover on His last earthly day.) Neither did the apostles of Christ, all Jews, nor His disciples, also all Jews.

But Jesus, who did the whole of His earthly teaching in Israel and in the Temple of Jerusalem, has disappeared from Jewish worship.

Instead, He is found in churches.

This, too, is well and good, and obviously has the blessing of the Messiah. But how has this Jew disappeared from our Jewish faith?

The fault doesn't lie entirely with the Gentiles. Because they have shown a hearty enthusiasm for the things of God and have aligned themselves with our Messiah does not convict them of removing Him from our worship.

We've done it ourselves, over the centuries.

Think about it: There was once a wholly Jewish group which honored Christ in Jerusalem. It is reviewed in the Book of Acts. Today, we Jews either ignore Christ, or receive Him and ignore Judaism.

But He remains with us in our unconscious worship, such as in the Passover, which honors Him. Why can't we come forward and stand united as Jews with our Messiah?

We do not have to "convert." We're already the Chosen People. We have merely to believe. When we believe in Jesus Christ we are truly the children of God.

As John recorded in His masterful book, "As many as received Him, to them He gave the right to become children of God" (1:12).

I have done this. I slowly acquainted myself with Jesus and considered our prophets. When I completely believed that He was the Messiah I became His follower.

And you know, my Jewish nose hasn't gotten any smaller, nor my hair any lighter. I still love a corned beef sandwich and an appetizer of chopped liver.

At the ABMJ mission where I worship, my Gentile Christian brethren serve up kosher foods, but, God bless them, they put pastrami on white bread and eat it with mayonnaise!

The day will never come when I take a pickle out of a glass jar and call it a "kosher dill." My reverence for matzoh balls does not permit me to refer to them as "dumplings."

I am completely a Jew. I never did observe all of our complex law, nor frequent the synagogue enough that they would know my name. But in the vital things of life which are Jewish, following the Messiah certainly hasn't changed me.

I remain a son of Levi, following the divine direction for my tribe given in Deuteronomy 10:8,9.

I have never been closer to God; not in seven years of Hebrew school, nor ten years of Sunday school, nor on the morning of my Bar Mitzvah. In fact, where God was a vague concept to me previously in my Jewish life, He is now my virtual Companion.

I don't know how I lived without Him.

Life with Christ is a deeply felt and significant life. It is not filled with wealth nor power, but with the simple virtues toward which these things are the desperate strivings. The Messiah said, "My peace I give unto you," and I can tell you that this alone makes life with Christ worthwhile.

Where I used to live in the midst of a busy argument between appetite and conscience, I now have standards and the strength to meet them. And I have an example in Jesus of a perfectly lived life.

I personally don't consider the message of Christ to be an emotional matter. I know people of all faiths who celebrate their gods with their feelings, ranging from ascetic silence to dancing and shouting. But to me the message of Christ is the fact of life. In His teachings is the answer to the great question, "What is truth?" This is the way things are in heaven and earth, and from the moment I adjusted to Christ's way, my life just seemed to blend into nature. I am now the creature God made, and I understand my place in all His creation.

The Lord said it best: "I am the way and the truth and the life" (John 14:6).

Now I do not fear even death. No one can harm me because God stands with me. What may pass for earthly trouble is always a part of God's plan, and I am being constantly perfected by Him.

I could gave umpteen examples of the little miracles I've seen. God doesn't send me burning bushes or angels, but He heals in a quiet way which testifies to His presence and His love.

And He is patient! If the apostle Paul was the "chief of sinners," as he said, then I sometimes feel at least next in line. Yet God stands by, sometimes with a rod, but always loving and faithful.

Words do not adequately describe the oneness with God that comes from believing in the Messiah. But it is a free gift of God, there for the taking, and presented "to the Jew first."

Brethren, I do not think I'll ever see my father again. None of us on earth is a judge of these things, but it would appear from the Scriptures that God will preserve only those who believed in His Son. God must be just.

I'll miss my father in the Kingdom to come. I don't want to miss you too. I am a Levite, separated by God to minister in His name and to bless my people. I do bless you, and I ask you to come to God.

Our Father has suffered with our suffering almost from the beginning of time. He asks so little now, and gives so great a reward.

Look at the first verse of the New Testament and see who our Messiah is. Come to Christ today.

Shalom.